GEORGE WASHINGTON CARVER

MASTERMINDS

IZZI HOWELL

B.E.S.

All inquiries should be addressed to:
Peterson's Publishing, LLC
4380 S. Syracuse Street, Suite 200
Denver, CO 80237-2624
www.petersonsbooks.com

ISBN: 978-1-4380-8905-8

Printed in China

All words in **bold** appear in the glossary on page 30.

Picture acknowledgements:
Alamy: Science History Images cover, 17 and 26; Getty: Stock Montage 4, duncan1890 7, Jupiterimages 9, Smith Collection/Gado 10, ilbusca 11, Photoquest 12, Bettmann 18 and 24, VCG Wilson/Corbis 21, DebbiSmirnoff 22t, Photo 12/ Universal Images Group 25, Mccallk69 27; Shutterstock: sunsetman 5, boreala 6t, Michael J. Munster 6b, Everett Historical 8 and 15, Smileus 13, Jeffrey M. Frank 14 and 28, Neil Bradfield 16, benjamas11 19, picturepartners, baibaz and elnavegante 22, Lili Blankenhship 23, catwalker 29l and 30, Michael Rega 29r, US Department of Agriculture (Public Domain) 20.
All design elements from Shutterstock.

Every effort has been made to clear copyright. Should there be any inadvertent omission, please apply to the publisher for rectification.

CONTENTS

WHO WAS GEORGE WASHINGTON CARVER?

George Washington Carver was an **agricultural** scientist. He helped to introduce new **crops** to the South, including peanuts, soybeans, and sweet potatoes.

During George Washington Carver's life, it was very unusual for African Americans to go to college or become scientists.

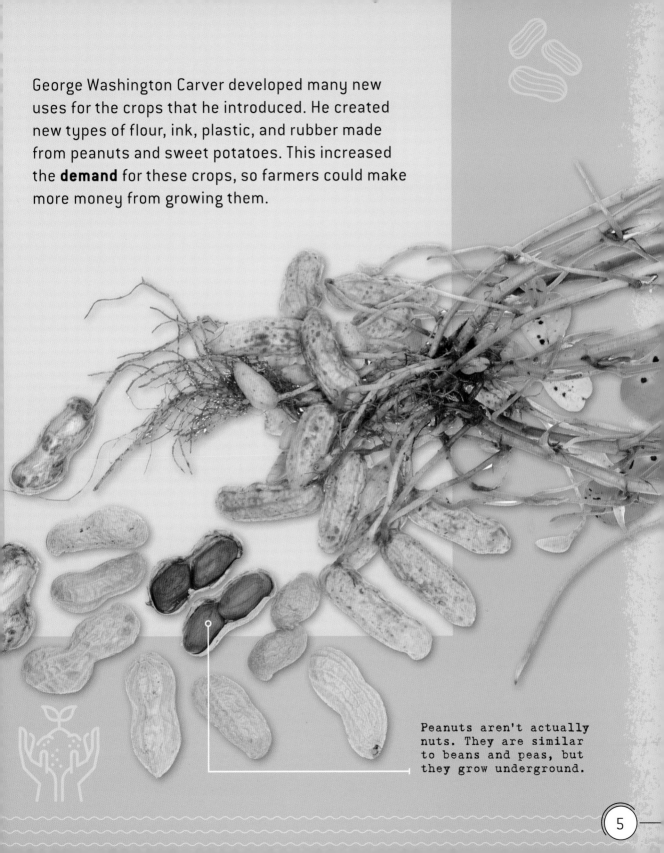

George Washington Carver developed many new uses for the crops that he introduced. He created new types of flour, ink, plastic, and rubber made from peanuts and sweet potatoes. This increased the **demand** for these crops, so farmers could make more money from growing them.

Peanuts aren't actually nuts. They are similar to beans and peas, but they grow underground.

George was born in the early 1860s near the town of Diamond, Missouri. His parents, Mary and Giles, were both **slaves**, which meant that George was a slave as well. Giles died before George was born. George's surname comes from Moses Carver—the man who owned the **plantation** where George lived.

Missouri

Today there is a monument to George Washington Carver on the farm where he grew up. This was Moses Carver's house. George, his mother, and several siblings lived in a simple log cabin with one room.

George was born during the Civil War (1861–65). This was a war between the northern and the southern **states**. One of the most important reasons for the war was that the North wanted to end slavery, but the South didn't.

During George's childhood, the farm on which he lived was **raided**. He was kidnapped, along with his mother and sister, and taken to Arkansas. Moses found George and brought him back, but he couldn't find George's mother or sister. George went on to grow up on the farm with his brother, James.

Many of the slaves in the South worked on cotton farms. It was very hard work and they were often treated badly.

The Civil War ended in 1865. Slavery was made illegal. This meant that George was no longer a slave.

In 1863, President Abraham Lincoln passed a law making slavery illegal in the North. After the Civil War ended, this became the law across the entire country.

However, it took a long time for slavery to end, even though it was now illegal. Plantation owners found other ways to make African Americans work for them for very little money.

George continued living on the plantation until he was about 12 years old. Moses and his wife, Susan, taught George how to read and write. He became interested in plants and local farmers called him "The Plant Doctor."

African American workers pick cotton on a plantation in 1914. Many African Americans continued working on plantations because they had no other way of making money and nowhere else to live.

Around the age of 12, George moved to a nearby town and started attending a school for black children. He lived with a family and helped them around the house in exchange for his room and food. However, the teachers at the school didn't have a lot of training. George wanted to learn more than they could teach him.

George attended a school for black children. White and black children had to attend different schools until the 1950s and 1960s.

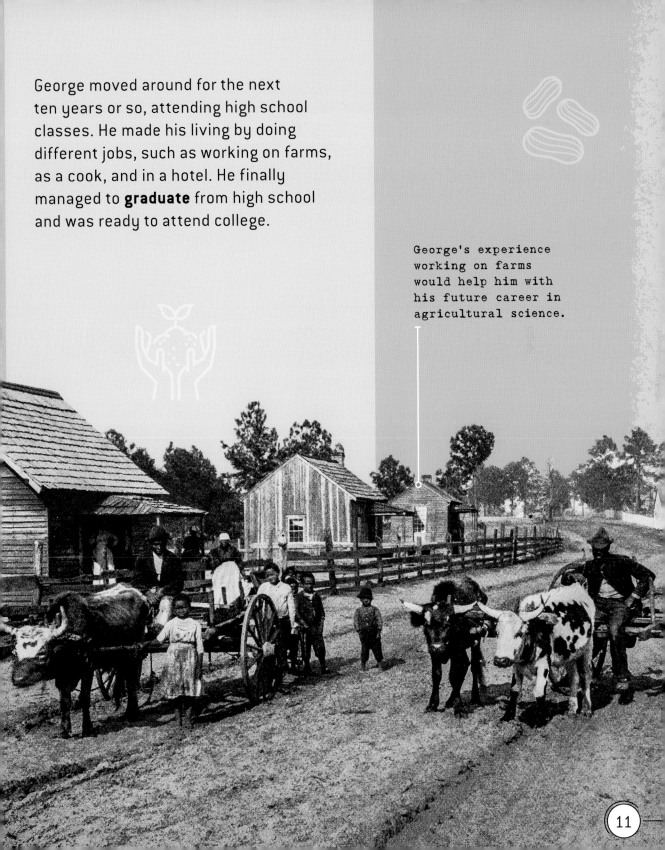

George moved around for the next ten years or so, attending high school classes. He made his living by doing different jobs, such as working on farms, as a cook, and in a hotel. He finally managed to **graduate** from high school and was ready to attend college.

George's experience working on farms would help him with his future career in agricultural science.

COLLEGE DAYS

The first college that George applied to rejected him because he was black. In 1890, he was given a place at Simpson College in Iowa. He studied art and piano.

George was a skilled artist. He painted all of his life, and some of his paintings won prizes.

George wasn't sure if he was going to be able to make a living from art. Instead, he chose to study farming because of his interest in plants. In 1891, he transferred to Iowa State Agricultural College.

George became the first African American to earn a **Bachelor of Science** degree. He followed this with a **master's degree**.

During his studies, George learned about soil, gardening, and farming techniques.

13

After graduating, many black colleges offered George work as a teacher. In 1896, he went to direct the new Department of Agriculture at the Tuskegee Institute in Alabama.

Tuskegee Institute still exists. Today it is known as Tuskegee University.

Booker T. Washington set up the Tuskegee Institute in 1881. He became its first **principal**. Booker wanted to improve the lives of African Americans through education. At his college, African American students learned farming and carpentry skills that they could use to earn a living. Many African Americans did not have these skills, as they had been forced to work as slaves.

Booker T. Washington helped to raise awareness of the issues affecting African Americans after slavery. He was born into slavery, but went on to work with the US government to help improve the lives of African Americans.

In the past, the area around the Tuskegee Institute had been used for slave plantations growing cotton. Over the years, this destroyed the soil because the cotton plants removed all of its **nutrients**. Very few plants could grow there.

As few plants grew in the soil, nothing held it together. Rain and wind easily **eroded** the soil, leaving huge ditches.

George did experiments to study the soil. He wanted to find out how farmers could add nutrients back into the soil so that they could grow crops again.

George collected soil samples in the fields to study back in his laboratory.

NEW CROPS

Finally, George found a solution to the soil problem. If farmers grew peanuts and soybeans, these plants would put the nutrient nitrogen back into the soil. These crops were also nutritious. Eating more peanuts and soybeans would help improve the health of poor African American farmers and their families.

African American farmers harvesting peanuts.

Another crop that George encouraged farmers to grow was sweet potatoes. They grew well in the soil of the South and produced lots of food. Growing sweet potatoes was an easy way for African American farmers to make money.

Sweet potatoes have a sweeter taste than regular potatoes and have pink or red skin.

At first, African American farmers weren't sure if they wanted to grow these new crops. Cotton had always been the crop that sold for the most money. There wasn't a huge demand for the new crops, which made them worried they would lose money if they planted them.

In 1906, George launched a **mobile** school that traveled around the countryside, educating farmers and helping them understand the benefits of the new crops.

THE BOOKER T. WASHINGTON
AGRICULTURAL SCHOOL ON WHEELS

George went back to his laboratory and worked on developing new products made from peanuts and sweet potatoes. If these crops could be used in many ways, there would be more demand for them. This would make farmers want to grow them.

peanut dye

peanut bread

peanut oil

peanut shaving cream

George developed around 300 uses for peanuts. Some were food products, such as peanut bread, peanut ice cream, and peanut coffee. Others were toiletries, such as face cream, shampoo, and soap. He also developed peanut laundry detergent, dyes, paints, inks, paper, and plastic.

George also developed over 100 uses for the sweet potato. These included flour, vinegar, glue for stamps, sugar, and cotton- and silk-like materials.

Carver sent out pamphlets to encourage farmers to grow his new crops. The pamphlets included instructions on how to make new products, such as soap, and recipes that they could make from these crops, such as sweet potato pie.

RESEARCH AND TEACHING

George's passion was **research**. He spent a huge amount of time in his laboratory, developing and testing his ideas. He was also an avid collector and gathered samples of many different species of plant.

George kept his plant collection at the Tuskegee Institute.

George also taught students at the Tuskegee Institute. As well as giving lessons in the classroom, George was a role model for many of the students. They had come from similar backgrounds to George, from poor families who had experienced slavery. George inspired them to continue with their education and work hard to achieve their dreams.

The Tuskegee Institute was one of a few colleges open to black students at this time.

George Washington Carver

George continued working at the Tuskegee Institute for the rest of his life. He worked on other important projects, such as finding replacements for 500 fabric dyes during the Second World War (1939–45). These dyes had previously been **imported** from Europe, but this wasn't possible during the war.

George had a lifelong love of painting. However, the only portrait he ever posed for was this painting, by Betsy Graves Reyneau, painted in 1942. He is shown with a new type of amaryllis flower that he had bred. George experimented with breeding other species of plant as well.

The gravestone reads:

GEORGE WASHINGTON CARVER
DIED IN TUSKEGEE ALABAMA
JANUARY 5, 1943

A LIFE THAT STOOD OUT AS A GOSPEL OF
SELF-FORGETTING SERVICE.
HE COULD HAVE ADDED FORTUNE TO FAME
BUT CARING FOR NEITHER HE FOUND HAPPI-
NESS AND HONOR IN BEING HELPFUL TO
THE WORLD.

THE CENTRE OF HIS WORLD WAS THE SOUTH
WHERE HE WAS BORN IN SLAVERY SOME
79 YEARS AGO AND WHERE HE DID HIS
WORK AS A CREATIVE SCIENTIST

George died on January 5, 1943 in Tuskegee, Alabama. He donated his life savings to the creation of the Carver Research Foundation to continue research in agriculture. Throughout his life, George had a huge impact on farming and education in the South and improved the lives of many African American farmers. George is quoted as saying, "Education is the key to unlock the golden door of freedom."

George was buried at the Tuskegee Institute, where he had spent most of his life.

The George Washington Carver Museum opened in 1941 at Tuskegee Institute. It contains samples of the products that George developed, as well as his collections of plants and paintings.

George's laboratory equipment is also on display at the George Washington Carver Museum.

The life and work of George Washington Carver have been celebrated in many ways. The monument built on the farm where he grew up was the first national monument dedicated to an African American. Schools and ships have been named after him, and his face has appeared on a half-dollar coin.

George has appeared on several stamps.

GLOSSARY

agricultural: Related to farming

bachelor of Science degree: An undergraduate degree in a science subject

crops: A plant that is grown in large quantities by farmers

demand: A need for an object to be supplied

erode: To wear away

graduate: To complete a high school or college course and receive a qualification

imported: Brought from another country

master's degree: A more advanced course of study at a college than an undergraduate degree

mobile: Able to be moved easily

nutrient: A substance that animals and humans need to eat, or plants need to take from the soil, to grow and stay alive

plantation: An area of land where crops are grown

principal: The person in charge of a school

raid: To attack a place and steal from it

research: Studying something in order to gather more information about it

slave: A person who is owned by someone else and forced to work for them for no money

TIMELINE

Early 1860s
George Washington Carver is born near Diamond, Missouri.

1865
The Civil War ends and slavery is made illegal.

1870s
George leaves the plantation to go to school, and later, high school.

1890
George studies art and piano at Simpson College in Iowa.

1891
George transfers to Iowa State Agricultural College to study farming.

FURTHER INFORMATION

BOOKS

STEM Scientists and Inventors: George Washington Carver by Mary Boone (Capstone, 2018)

Who Was George Washington Carver? by Jim Gigliotti (Penguin Workshop, 2015)

Great Black Heroes: Five Brilliant Scientists by Lynda Jones (Scholastic, 2000)

WEBSITES

www.tuskegee.edu/support-tu/ george-washington-carver Informative website from the college where George Washington Carver taught.

www.nationalpeanutboard.org/ news/16-surprising-facts-about- george-washington-carver.htm Discover 16 fun facts about George Washington Carver.

www.history.com/topics/black- history/george-washington-carver Read a biography of George Washington Carver.

1896
George begins work in the Department of Agriculture at the Tuskegee Institute in Alabama.

1906
George launches a mobile school to educate farmers about the benefits of new crops, such as peanuts, sweet potatoes, and soybeans.

1940s
George finds replacements for 500 fabric dyes during the Second World War.

1941
The George Washington Carver Museum opens at the Tuskegee Institute.

1943
George dies and is buried at the Tuskegee Institute.

INDEX

More titles in the the **Masterminds** series

- Who was Rachel Carson? • Childhood
- University life • Under the sea • Writing and books • Marine research • Pesticides
- Silent Spring
- Speaking out • Death
- The green movement
- Remembering Rachel Carson • Our environment today

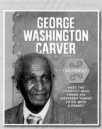

- Who was George Washington Carver?
- Childhood • Freedom
- Getting an education
- Farm studies • New crops • Peanut products
- The sweet potato
- Making a change
- Colourful dyes
- Honours • Later life
- Remembering Carver

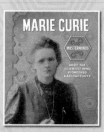

- Who was Marie Curie?
- Childhood • Studies in France • Meeting Pierre • Studying rays
- New discoveries
- Radioactive radium
- Working hard • Family
- Teaching and learning
- The First World War
- Later years
- Remembering Marie Curie

- Who was Rosalind Franklin? • Childhood
- University • The Second World War
- Working in France
- DNA • A new job
- Photographic evidence
- Studying viruses
- Forgotten work
- Illness • Celebrating Rosalind Franklin

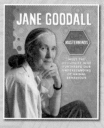

- Who is Jane Goodall?
- Childhood • Off to Africa • Ancestors and evolution • Living with chimpanzees • New discoveries • Back to school • Family
- Inspiring others
- Books • The Jane Goodall Institute
- Activism • Celebrating Jane Goodall

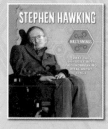

- Who was Stephen Hawking? • Childhood
- University days
- Family • Space-time study • Black holes
- A new voice • Sharing science • The future
- Adventures • *The Theory of Everything*
- Awards • Remembering Stephen Hawking

- Who is Katherine Johnson? • Bright beginnings • Getting ahead • Teaching and family • A new job
- Fighting prejudice
- Into space • In orbit
- To the Moon • Later life
- *Hidden Figures*
- Celebrating Katherine Johnson • A new generation

- Who was Nikola Tesla?
- Childhood • Growing up
- Electricity and Edison
- Moving to the USA
- Branching out • The war of the currents
- New projects
- Wireless power
- Struggles • Awards
- Later life
- Remembering Tesla

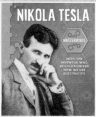

- Who was Leonardo da Vinci? • Early life
- Working in Milan
- Famous paintings
- Body sketches • Back to Florence • The Mona Lisa • Animal sketches
- Flight sketches
- Military sketches
- Engineering sketches
- The later years
- Remembering Leonardo

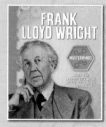

- Who was Frank Lloyd Wright? • Childhood
- Education • Off to Chicago • Family • First designs • Prairie houses
- Building details
- A new home
- Teaching • Famous buildings • Later life
- Remembering Frank Lloyd Wright